~ *Craft Ideas for Your Home* ~

PILLOWMAKING

~ Craft Ideas for Your Home ~

PILLOWMAKING

CANDIE FRANKEL

Little, Brown and Company
Boston   New York   Toronto   London

To Mom, who taught me how and why

~

Acknowledgments

*The author gratefully acknowledges the many fine photographers and
designers whose work is featured in these pages.*

~

First edition

ISBN 0-316-29167-6

Library of Congress Catalogue Card Number 94-77000

A FRIEDMAN GROUP BOOK

10 9 8 7 6 5 4 3 2 1

Published simultaneously in Canada by Little, Brown & Company (Canada) Limited

CRAFT IDEAS FOR YOUR HOME: PILLOWMAKING
was prepared and produced by
Michael Friedman Publishing Group
15 West 26th Street
New York, New York 10010

Editor: Elizabeth Viscott Sullivan
Art Director: Jeff Batzli
Designer: Lynne Yeamans
Layout: Ed Noriega
Photography Editor: Colleen Branigan
Production Associate: Camille Lee
Illustrator: Barbara Hennig

Printed and bound in China

Contents

~

Introduction

$\mathcal{S}$ewing your own pillows is one of the fastest, most economical ways to transform the decor of your home. Pillows pack tremendous power for their size. They can infuse a room with zingy colors, underscore subtle tone-on-tone schemes, and introduce novelty trims and sewing techniques. Pillows are masters of disguise, playfully suggesting different climates, cultures, or historical periods without the fuss—and expense—of redecorating an entire room.

As decorating accents, pillows provide important clues to a room's personality. Large lounging pillows that can be moved about the room invite guests to make themselves at home or stretch out on the couch. Expensive fabrics, delicate laces, and hand needlework impart a more formal, elegant ambience. When the decor is eclectic, pillows can help balance disparate furnishings and textiles by echoing key motifs and colors. Some pillows are designed strictly for the exquisite or exotic accent they bestow on an interior, but most pillows are soft and resilient enough to offer function as well as style.

Assembled from just a few pieces of fabric, stuffing, and decorative trims, pillows are incredibly easy to sew and embellish. Home sewers can create imitations of designer and one-of-a-kind pillows for a fraction of their markup cost in home furnishings stores. Beginning sewing skills are all you need to get started, since even the most lavish applications are variations on a few basic styles. By choosing your own fabrics and trims, you can create pillows in the colors, shapes, and sizes that suit your decorating vision instead of settling for the predictable, look-alike designs and color palettes available commercially. The instructions and tips that follow will teach you not only how to sew the most basic styles but also how to stretch and adapt your skills so that you can bring all of your design ideas to successful completion.

Sewing Equipment

Pillowmaking requires basic sewing equipment and supplies. In addition to fabric, thread, trims, and stuffing, which are discussed in the sections that follow, you will need a sewing machine, hand-sewing needles, straight pins, scissors, a seam ripper, a tape measure, and fabric marking pens to complete your pillow projects. A rotary cutter, while not essential, is of great advantage. A brief description of each item follows. If you have never sewn before, or sew only infrequently, the descriptions will guide you both in assembling the supplies you need and in using them to best advantage.

Sewing Machine While pillows can be sewn by hand, the work will go much faster and with less effort if you use a sewing machine. Pillows experience great tension at the seams because of the stuffing. The small, equally spaced stitches produced by a sewing machine help distribute the tension evenly, so the seams don't open up. You don't need a fancy machine, and you don't need to be a whiz at using it. To sew a straight line, use the seam guide on the metal plate to the lower right of the needle. If your machine is old and no guide is present, lay down a piece of tape so that its left edge is exactly ¹/₂" to the right of the needle plate hole. As you feed the fabric under the needle, align the edge of the fabric against the edge of the tape to make perfect ¹/₂" seams. For pucker-free seams, use the proper size needle in the machine: size 12 (80mm) for medium-weight fabrics, such as cotton and linen, and size 14 (90mm) for slightly heavier fabrics, such as upholstery weights and fabric cut from old bedspreads.

Hand-Sewing Needles

Buy a package of sharps—the universal hand-sewing needle—in assorted sizes. You will use hand-sewing needles for basting and to close up a pillow after the stuffing or pillow form is inserted. Any size from the package that feels comfortable to you is fine for the small amount of hand sewing you will need to do.

Pins

Straight pins are used to hold pieces of fabric and trims together temporarily until they are sewn. A small box of stainless steel pins will see you through many sewing projects, though you may prefer longer pins, sometimes called quilter's pins, for holding thick or bulky fabrics and trims. Some pins are manufactured with small plastic or glass balls covering the heads, which makes them easier to see and to handle.

Rotary Cutter and Accessories

A rotary cutter consists of a thin, round, razor-sharp blade attached to the end of a plastic handle. The user holds the handle and rolls the blade along the fabric surface like a wheel, cutting through the fabric in one continuous motion. To make straight cuts, the blade is rolled along the edge of a clear plastic cutting

guide that is typically imprinted with standard measurements. The work surface is protected by a self-healing cutting mat that is placed underneath the fabric. The rotary cutter and its accessories are especially useful tools for measuring and cutting the square and rectangular pieces of fabric used in pillowmaking. They provide accurate cuts in a fraction of the time needed to mark fabric with a marking pen and cut it with scissors.

Scissors

Even if you have a rotary cutter, you will still need scissors. Scissors are used in pillowmaking to cut loose thread ends, trim off corners, and snip away excess trim and piping to reduce bulk. Scissors should be sharp and should open and close freely. If you plan to do a lot of sewing, you may wish to purchase high-quality sewing shears. To protect the blades, be sure to use sewing shears only to cut fabric, never to cut paper or for household chores.

Seam Ripper

When you need to pick out a few stitches—for instance, to open up a casing for a gathered-end bolster or to

correct some irregular stitching—you will save time and avoid frustration by using a seam ripper. The point of the seam ripper slips right under or in between the stitches, and its sharp edge cuts the thread with a quick snap. Methods using scissors or the point of a pin simply aren't worth the time or effort.

Tape Measure

A flexible fiberglass tape measure, unlike rigid metal or wood rulers, lets you take accurate measurements of curved pillow forms. Choose a tape measure that is marked on both sides so that you can simply flip it over if you pick it up at the wrong end.

Fabric Marking Pens

Fabric marking pens are useful for marking cutting lines, corner pivot points, and the sections to be left open for turning and stuffing. Some pen marks are formulated to evaporate after 12 to 24 hours, while others are designed to wash out. When using marking pens, always test the pen on a sample of the fabric you will be using and make sure the mark comes out before you use the pen in the actual pillow.

Basic Pillow Forms and How to Make Them

~

The foundation of every pillow is a form that fits inside the pillow cover to give it its shape and volume. Basic pillow shapes include squares, rectangles, circles, and sausagelike bolsters. You can buy manufactured pillow forms in these shapes in a range of sizes, or you can make them yourself. Novelty shapes such as hearts, ovals, triangles, and spheres are also possibilities. Most manufactured forms are made of spun polyester or high-density foam, both of which are long-lasting and spring back when crushed, although high-density foam is more rigid and has less give. For a heftier, plusher, more luxurious pillow, choose a loose natural filling, such as feathers and down. Ready-made pillow forms and stuffing materials are sold at craft and sewing supply stores as well as through upholsterers and foam suppliers, all of which can be easily found through the phone book.

To create a custom-size pillow, you must make the form yourself. Forms that will be stuffed with polyester filling can be sewn from plain muslin or a similar woven fabric. Feathers and down require a high-thread-count fabric, such as an old, clean sheet, which will prevent the feather spurs from poking through the weave but will still allow the filling to breathe. Feathers and down are wispy, flyaway, and very difficult to manipulate, so unless you have experience and patience, you are better off letting a professional fill the form for you. If you have feathers and down from an old pillow that you would like to recycle, a professional bedding service can clean them, fluff them up, and insert them in casings that you provide.

There are three basic pillow forms: knife-edged, boxing strip, and dimensional. Knife-edged pillows are "flat"—two pieces of fabric are sewn together and the filling is sandwiched between them. When a boxing strip (a long, narrow piece of fabric) is used to connect the pillow front and back, the knife edge disappears and the pillow takes on a stockier, heftier look. Dimensional pillows depart from this construction entirely, and they include rolled bolsters and novelty shapes such as spheres. The following brief instructions will show you how easy it is to create these different forms, each of which can be the base for a decorative pillow cover that you sew later.

Knife-Edged Pillow Forms

To make a knife-edged form 15" square, cut two squares of fabric each 16" by 16", or 1" larger than the desired finished size (A). Place the pieces right sides together and machine-stitch $1/2$" from the edges, leaving a 7"–8" opening on one side. Clip diagonally across the corners, then turn the form cover right side out (B).

Pull a clump of polyester filling from the packaging, fluff it out with your fingers, and insert it into the opening. Continue stuffing the form, taking care to fill the corners and distribute the filling evenly. When the entire pillow is filled and firm, whipstitch the opening closed. Use this same technique to make any knife-edged form, including rectangular, circular, triangular, and heart shapes.

9
~

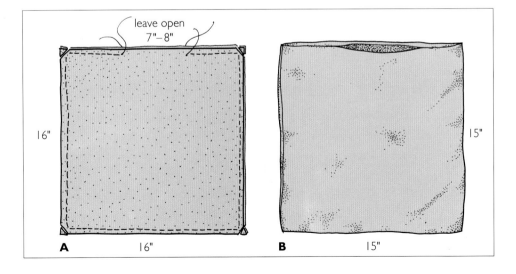

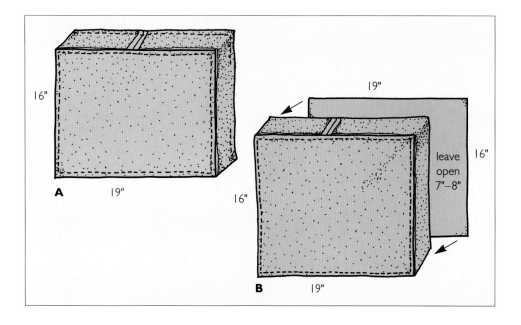

16"

19"

A

19"

16"

19"

leave
open
7"–8"

16"

B

19"

Boxing Strip Pillow Forms

To make a box-edged form 15" by 18", cut two rectangles of fabric, each 16" by 19", or 1" larger than the desired finished size. Cut a boxing strip 67" long, or the perimeter of the finished pillow plus 1". The boxing strip width can vary from 2" to 6", depending on the pillow design; always cut the strip 1" larger than the desired finished width to allow for ½" seams.

To assemble the pillow, first sew the two short ends of the boxing strip together in a ½" seam, then press the seam open. You should have a continuous loop. Place an edge of the boxing strip against one edge of a fabric rectangle, right sides together, and secure with pins. With the boxing strip on top, machine-stitch through both layers ½" from the edges, stopping ½" from the corner with the needle down in the fabric. Lift the presser foot, pivot the work 90 degrees, and smooth the excess box-

ing strip to the back. Lower the presser foot and continue sewing through both layers ½" from the edge, turning the remaining corners in the same way (A). Sew the second rectangle to the other edge of the boxing strip in the same manner, taking care to align the corners (B). Leave a 7"–8" opening along one edge. Turn and stuff as for the knife-edged pillow.

Dimensional Pillow Forms

Bolster To roll your own bolster form, choose a piece of 2"-thick, high-density foam 18"–24" wide (or the desired length of the finished bolster) and 24"–36" long. Beginning at a short end, roll the foam tightly, holding it securely with both hands as you go. When you reach the end, ask a partner to tie string tightly around the roll every 6" to keep it from spring-

ing open (A). Cut a sheet of cotton batting that is 2" longer than the roll and three times its circumference (the circular distance around the roll). Wrap the batting around the roll (you should be able to make three complete wraps) and whipstitch the loose edge. Fold the excess over the ends (B).

To cover the bolster form, cut a piece of fabric that is 1" longer than the padded bolster and that will wrap around it once plus 1". Sew the edges together to make a tube and turn right side out. Using an iron, press the raw edges at each end ½" to the inside. Pull this skin onto the form, taking care not to shift or dislodge the batting underneath. Cut two fabric circles the diameter of each end plus 1". Place a circle over each end, tuck the edges underneath the pressed edge, and slip-stitch in place (C).

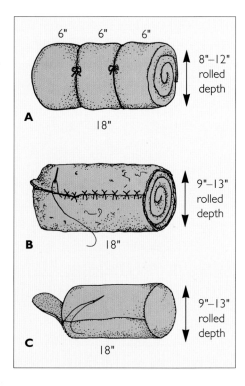

6"   6"   6"

8"–12"
rolled
depth

A

18"

9"–13"
rolled
depth

B

18"

9"–13"
rolled
depth

C

18"

Sphere A spherical, or globe-shaped, pillow form is made by sewing six leaf-shaped pieces of fabric together. To draw the leaf-shaped pattern, you will need a large chalkboard drafting compass, a clear plastic ruler, a large sheet of paper, and a pencil. If you don't have a large compass, you can improvise with string, a pushpin, and a pencil. Tie a knot in one end of the string and insert the pushpin point through the knot down onto the paper to represent the compass point. Tie a second knot so that the distance between the knots equals the desired radius and slip the pencil point into it. To draw the arc, move the point of the pencil along the paper, being sure to keep the string taut.

To begin, you must decide on the finished circumference, or the distance around the pillow—typically somewhere between 30" and 40". If you have trouble visualizing a finished size, hold a tape measure in a ring as if you were measuring a waistline, adjust the ring larger or smaller until you find the size you prefer, then read the circumference directly off the tape. Divide the circumference by 4, set the compass to that radius, and draw a circle. To make a pillow form with a 36" circumference, for example, you would draw a circle with a radius that measures one fourth of 36", or 9". Draw perpendicular vertical and horizontal lines through the center of the circle, dividing the area into four equal pie-shaped wedges. Extend the horizontal lines I" on each side (A).

To create the basic leaf shape, set the compass point on the right end of the horizontal line. Extend the compass so the lead touches the vertical line intersection at the top

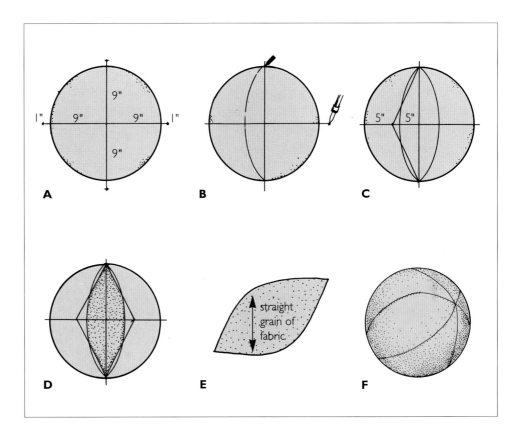

of the circle. Draw an arc from this point through the interior to the lower circle edge (B). Repeat this step from the left side to complete the symmetrical pattern.

To refine the pattern, measure the left horizontal line segment between the endpoint and the circle center, and mark the midpoint. In the example for the 36" pillow, the midpoint would divide the line into two 5" segments. Draw a straight line connecting the midpoint to the top and bottom leaf points (C). Repeat on the opposite side for a diamond shape. Cut out the pattern on the inside straight and curved lines (D). Fold the completed pattern in fourths along the marked lines, then taper the pattern edge where the straight and curved lines meet by cutting

through all four layers. Fold the pattern in half one more time (into eighths), crease sharply, then unfold. Use the pattern to cut six shapes from fabric, laying the diagonal crease along the straight grain of the fabric (E).

Join three fabric pieces together by sewing along the long curved edges, making ¼" seams. Reinforce each seam after you sew it by topstitching through all layers. Assemble the remaining three pieces in the same way. Join the two halves of the sphere together, matching the top and bottom points and leaving a 4"–5" opening along one side. Turn right side out and stuff firmly by maneuvering the filling out to the edges and inserting new filling into the center of the sphere. When the form is fully stuffed, whipstitch the opening closed (F).

Choosing Fabric

Once you have purchased or made a pillow form in the size and shape of your choosing, your next step is to cover the pillow. Just about any new or rejuvenated textile can be used. Sturdy weights and weaves of silk, linen, or wool are hard-wearing choices for living rooms, libraries, hallways, family rooms, and similar areas that receive daily use. Decorator upholstery cottons are likewise long-wearing and let you introduce a variety of prints, plaids, and stripes to the decor of a room. If you like the retro look, fabrics recycled from old drapes and slipcovers are well worth seeking out for their gently dulled softness. More delicate textiles, such as lace, eyelet, gauze, and lightweight cottons, lend a feminine aura to bedrooms and quiet sitting areas. Generally, it's best not to cover pillows with rare, valuable, or extremely fragile textiles because of the potential for damage through ordinary wear and tear.

When you shop, look for durable light- to medium-weight fabrics rather than the heaviest weights, which can stress the motor of your sewing machine. Always choose the best-quality fabric you can afford, and to develop your eye, take time to examine interesting weaves, textures, and natural fibers up close. Do not compromise your own aesthetic judgment, for when you work with a fabric that you truly love, you will be more attentive to details and your finished work will look more professional.

To prepare both new and old fabrics for sewing, run them through the appropriate washing machine and dryer cycles to shrink the fabric and remove any sizing or dirt. If the fabric seems fragile, such as lace, soak it by hand in warm, sudsy water and rinse it well in cool water, but do not subject it to washing-machine agitation. You can dry hand-washed fabrics in a dryer set to a delicate cycle, or lay the fabric flat on toweling to dry. Press out any wrinkles with a steam iron before you measure the fabric for sewing.

Sewing Pillow Covers

The key to a superb pillow cover is a firm fit. Pillows with forms that slosh around inside their covers look unpleasantly baggy, not to mention sloppy, and tend to crinkle up and collapse when you lean against them. To prevent this problem, it is critical that the finished pillow cover be sized slightly smaller than the pillow form. To cut the cover fabric in the proper size, measure the form both horizontally and vertically, using a tape measure rather than a ruler to follow the contours accurately, then add $1/2$" to each measurement. A 15"-square knife-edged pillow form, for example, would require two $15 1/2$" squares of cover fabric. When these two pieces are sewn together with $1/2$" seams, the resulting cover is $14 1/2$" square, or $1/2$" smaller than the pillow form. Once the form is inserted, the cover stretches taut over it, resulting in a plump pillow that springs back into shape easily and resists wrinkling.

The following instructions will guide you in measuring, cutting, and sewing a variety of cover styles to fit knife-edged forms, forms with boxing strips, and dimensional forms. Sample measurements are sometimes included to help you visualize the construction and see how to substitute the measurements for your project. If you have difficulty inserting a commercial-spun polyester pillow form into a cover because the burrlike fibers catch on the fabric, sew a separate muslin cover for the form before placing it into the cover following the pillow form instructions on page 9.

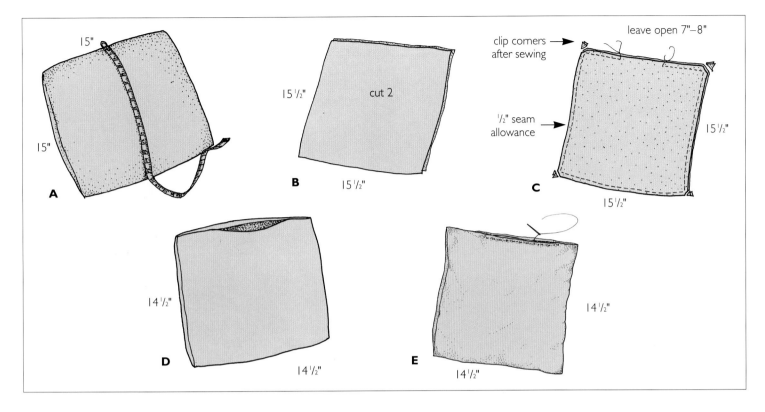

Covers for Knife-Edged Pillows

Basic Cover

Measure the form (A), then cut two fabric pieces—front and back—that are ½" larger than the form dimensions (B). Place the pieces together, right sides facing. Machine-stitch ½" from the edges all around, leaving a 7"–8" opening in one side. Clip diagonally across the corners (C). Turn the cover right side out, and use a crewel embroidery needle to pick out the points at the corners so that they are sharp and crisp (D). Insert the form into the cover and manipulate it with your fingers so that it fills out the space. Ease the form away from the opening and pin the opening closed ½" from the edge. Slip-stitch with matching sewing thread, then remove the pins (E).

Cover with Turkish Corners

This variation on the basic knife-edged pillow cover has rounded corners for a softer look. After machine-stitching the basic cover with opening, wrap and tie the four corners with heavy-duty thread 1"–2" in from each point (A). Turn the cover right side out, insert the form, and slip-stitch the opening closed (B). You can also tie off Turkish corners after the cover is turned to the right side.

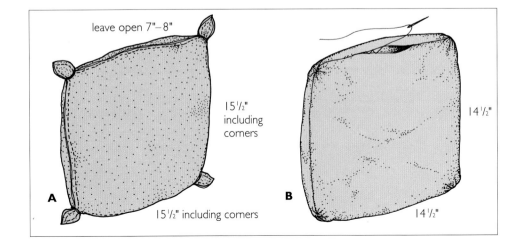

Cover with Flange Edge The flange edge is a tailored finish suitable for square and rectangular knife-edged pillows. A flange is a flat, ornamental flap of fabric that extends beyond the pillow form evenly on all sides. Flanges are typically 2"–4" wide and are most effective with crisp, lightweight fabrics such as linen and cotton. To reduce bulk along the outer edges, the cover is cut in one piece in a diamond shape and sewn so that the seams form an X pattern on the back. The same method is used to make both square and rectangular covers, though the latter requires some fabric manipulation to get the seams right. If you have never sewn a flange-edged pillow cover before, make your first one for a square pillow, which will help you better understand the construction.

To begin, you must determine the dimensions of the finished pillow cover including flanges by adding two flange widths to the pillow form length and width. A cover with a 3" flange for a 15"-square pillow, for example, would measure 3" plus 3" plus 15" by 3" plus 3" plus 15", or 21" by 21". To determine the dimensions of the fabric diamond from which you will sew the cover, double the pillow dimensions, then add 1". In our example, the diamond would measure 21" plus 21" plus 1" by 21" plus 21" plus 1", or 43" by 43". These two dimensions will always be the same when the pillow is square, but they will be different when the pillow is a rectangle.

To cut the diamond, start with a piece of fabric slightly larger than the diamond dimensions. Fold the fabric in quarters by folding it in half once along the lengthwise grain, then once along the crosswise grain. Pin the four layers together close to the folds to keep them from shifting. Starting at the folded corner, measure along one edge for one half of the diamond length and mark it with a pin. Mark the other folded edge in the same way for one-half the diamond width. Lay the fabric on a cutting mat, place a cutting guide on top to mark a diagonal line connecting the two pin marks, and cut through all layers against the guide with a rotary cutter (A) (G). If you don't have a rotary cutter, you can draw a straight line between the pins with a marking pen and cut along the line with scissors. Open up the folds to see the diamond (B) (H).

To assemble the cover, bring two adjacent points of the diamond together, right

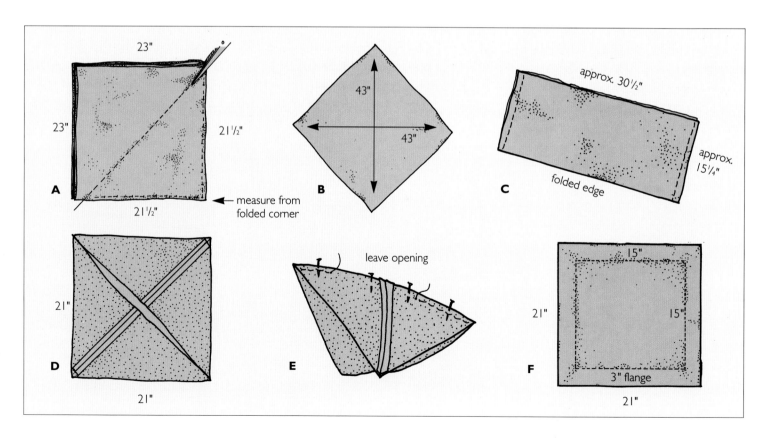

A 23" 23" 21½" 21½" ← measure from folded corner

B 43" 43"

C approx. 30½" approx. 15¼" folded edge

D 21" 21"

E leave opening

F 15" 15" 21" 3" flange 21"

sides in and edges matching, and sew with a $1/2$" seam. Repeat for the two other corners. If you are sewing a cover for a square pillow, simply fold the diamond in half to form a rectangle to complete this step (C). If you are sewing a cover for a rectangular pillow, the fabric will assume an awkward popped-up rectangular shape during this step (I). When you have sewn both seams, open out the shape and press the seams open (D) (J). You should be able to see the X-shaping of the seams emerging. Open out the shape again and pin the remaining raw edges together, right sides facing and seamlines matching. Stitch from each corner in toward the center for about 5", leaving an opening in the center for turning (E) (K). Press the seams and the excess fabric at the opening to one side. Turn the cover right side out.

To sew the flange edge, hand-baste 3" (or the desired flange width) in from all four edges, measuring as you sew to check your accuracy. Machine-stitch around the pillow perimeter on the basting lines. Remove the basting thread (F) (L). Insert the pillow form into the opening at the back and slip-stitch closed.

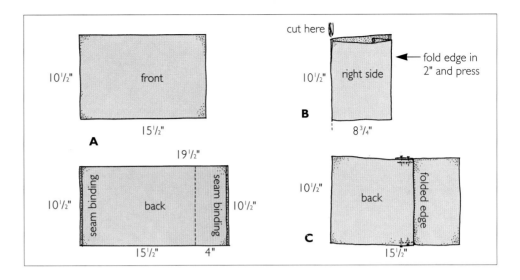

Sham A sham is a cover that slips over the pillow form through a flaplike opening at the back. To make a sham, cut one front $1/2$" larger than the form (just like the basic knife-edged cover) and one back the same width as the front but 4" longer. A front for a 10" by 15" form, for example, would be $10 1/2$" by $15 1/2$", and the back would be $10 1/2$" by $15 1/2$" plus 4", or $10 1/2$" by $19 1/2$" (A).

To assemble the sham, first finish both short edges of the pillow back with purchased seam binding (A). Fold one short edge 2" to the wrong side and press. Fold the entire back piece in half, matching the folded and bound edges, and press. Cut on the second fold, for two pieces (B). Lay both pieces right side up on a flat surface. Lap the folded edge 2" over the bound edge, or so that the overall length matches the front piece. Pin the overlaps at the edges, then machine-baste (C). To finish, assemble the sham front and back as for a knife-edged pillow.

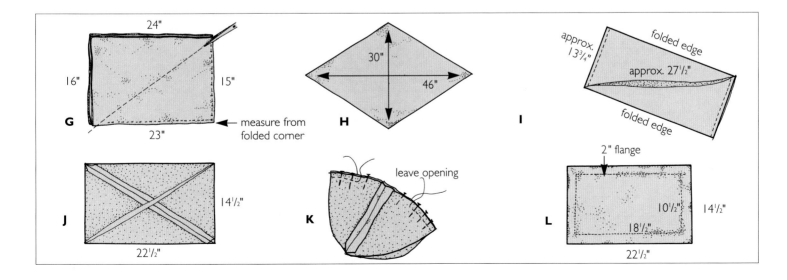

Installing Zipper Closings

Zippers are worth installing if you anticipate cleaning your pillow covers frequently or if you are making several pillow covers that you would like to rotate. Choose a zipper and thread color that matches the predominant color in the cover fabric. Use the sewing machine's zipper foot attachment instead of the standard presser foot for smooth, even stitching near the zipper teeth and pull.

In Knife-Edged Covers

Zippers for square and rectangular knife-edged styles should be 2"–3" shorter than one finished side edge. Cut one dimension of the front and back covers ¹/₄" larger, for a ⁵/₈" seam allowance (instead of ¹/₂") on the zipper side. Place the covers together, right sides facing and edges matching. Machine-baste ⁵/₈" from the edge only on the side where the zipper will be installed.

Open out the pieces and enclose the zipper in the seam following the zipper package directions (A). After the zipper is installed, refold the cover right side in and sew the three remaining sides together with a ¹/₂" seam (B). Slide the zipper open, turn the pillow cover right side out, insert the form through the opening, and zip the cover closed (C).

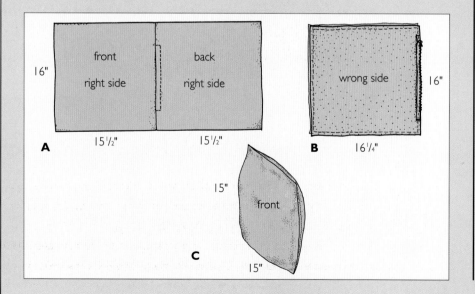

In Boxing Strips

Unlike knife-edged pillows, in which the zipper falls between two corners, covers with boxing strips are easier to remove if the zipper extends slightly around the pillow corners. Some additional steps are required to install the zipper, but the result is a well-tailored look.

To begin, measure the width and length of the boxing strip on the pillow form. Add ¹/₂" to the width and 1" to the length, and jot down the results. Label the new width X and the new length Y. Choose a zipper that is 4" longer than the shorter pillow side. Add 1¹/₂" to the zipper measurement to obtain length Z.

Cut a boxing strip that is X plus 1¹/₄" wide by Z. Cut the strip in half lengthwise, then machine-baste the edges together to make a ⁵/₈" seam. Center the zipper on the seam and sew following the zipper package directions (A). The width of the zippered strip should equal X.

Cut a second boxing strip X wide by Y minus Z plus 1" long. Sew the short ends to the ends of the zippered strip, making ¹/₂" seams. You should have a continuous loop with a circumference equal to Y.

Sew the completed boxing strip to the pillow front and back, right sides facing, as described on page 10, taking care to position the zipper so it spans one end of the pillow (B). Turn the cover to the right side, insert the pillow form, and zip closed (C).

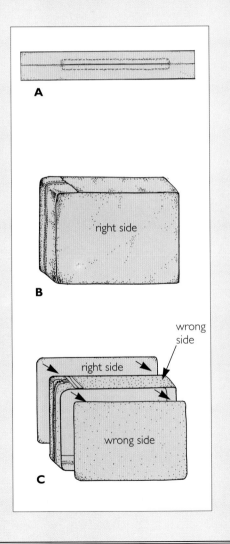

A

B

right side

C

right side

wrong side

wrong side

Cover with a Boxing Strip

Measure and cut the cover front and back 1" larger than the pillow form. Measure and cut the boxing strip ½" wider and 1" longer than the finished boxing strip on the pillow form. Sew as for a pillow form with boxing strip (page 10).

Covers for Dimensional Pillows

Bolster Cover with Gathered Ends
This elegant bolster cover is easy to sew. It is made from just one piece of fabric, and you will need to take three measurements to figure the dimensions: length (X), circumference (Y), and diameter (Z).

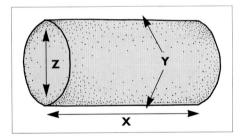

Measure and cut a rectangle X plus Z plus 1" long by Y plus ½" wide. Fold the rectangle in half, right side in and X-Z edges matching, and sew the X-Z edges together in a ½" seam. Fold the short raw edges ¾" to the wrong side and press. Machine-stitch ½" from each fold to create a casing at each end (A). Pick out a few stitches on the long seam to gain access to the casing and run a length of string or ribbon through the casing using a large blunt-pointed tapestry needle (B). Turn the cover right side out and pull it over the pillow form. Pull the drawstrings to gather each end in a tight ring. Tie the string ends together, and tuck them inside. If the pillow form is visible, insert a small square of matching or contrasting fabric behind the opening to conceal it (C). The tight gathering will hold it in place without stitching. If you wish, you can pull the fabric slightly out of the opening to create a small pouf.

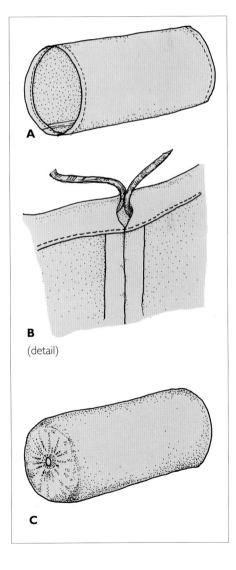

A

B
(detail)

C

Bolster Cover with Pancake End

This bolster is more tailored than the gathered bolster just described, but it uses the same measurements. Cut one rectangle A plus 1" long by B plus 1/2" wide and two circles C plus 1" in diameter. Sew the pieces together as described in the instructions for the bolster pillow form cover (page 10).

Cover for a Sphere

Pillow covers for spheres can be made in a single solid color, or each wedge can be cut from a different color for a beach-ball effect. Cut and assemble the pieces following the pillow form instructions (page 11). For a proper fit and to reinforce the seams, sew each seam 1/4" and again 5/16" from the edge; topstitching is optional, depending on the type of tailoring you desire. Leave a 9"–12" opening, and staystitch 5/16" from each open edge before you insert the form to prevent stretching. Punch down and compress the pillow form as tightly as you can when inserting it. Slip-stitch the pillow closed, concealing the staystitching.

Trims and Embellishments

Beautiful fabrics are only part of a pillow's attractiveness. Trims and embellishments can stress a particular color, introduce new fibers and textures, or augment a rich, opulent fabric. Trims such as cord, piping, and fringe that are sewn into or over the seams can highlight a pillow's shape or soften a hard knife-edge. Other trims, including buttons, beads, sequins, and tassels, can be sewn directly to the surface of the pillow cover to achieve an elegant or whimsical surface decoration. The instructions that follow show how to install basic trims; you can use the same principles and measurements when you are ready to try some of your own designs.

Piping

Piping, or welting, provides a neat, tailored finish that is especially effective along boxing strip seams. You can make piping yourself in the fabric of your choice, or you can purchase it ready-made in packages or by the yard. Commercial trim featuring a barrel-shaped cord on a flat binding is applied the same way as piping.

Making Piping

Piping is made with piping cord filler, available in various diameters at notions counters. Generally, a 1/4"-diameter cord works well, but you may want a thicker cord for extra-large pillows or to accent heavier fabrics. You will also need a large square of fabric for covering the cord. The fabric strips used to cover the cord are cut on the bias (diagonal), which has a slight stretch, allowing the finished piping to turn corners smoothly

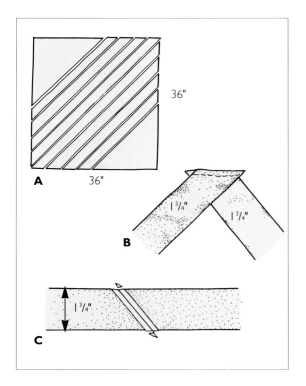

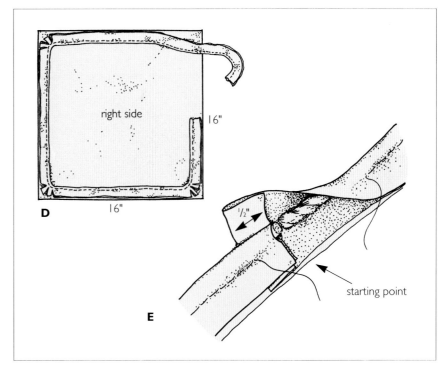

when it is sewn to the pillow top. Generally, several strips must be joined together for a piece that is long enough to sew around the perimeter of the pillow.

To make the piping, cut a 36" square of fabric diagonally from corner to corner, then make adjacent parallel cuts to form the bias strips (A). You can use a ruler, marking pen, and scissors to mark and cut the strips, but a rotary cutter, cutting guide, and cutting mat will give more accurate results and make the job go faster. To determine the width of the strips, multiply the cord diameter by 3, then add 1"; for a $1/4$" cord, for example, you would need strips measuring $1/4$" times 3 plus 1", or $1^3/4$" wide. Cut as many strips as necessary to exceed the pillow perimeter, remembering to double the amount for a boxing strip cover that will be piped front and back. Trim off the selvages, then place the short edges together,

right sides facing, and machine-stitch (B). Press the seams open and trim off the excess (C). Place the long strip wrong side up, then lay piping cord filler along the center. Fold the strip over the cord so the long raw edges match. Using the zipper foot attachment for your sewing machine instead of the regular presser foot, machine-baste (sew long stitches) through both layers close to the cord without pinching or crowding it. The zipper foot design allows the sewing machine needle to stitch closer to the bulky cord than the standard presser foot used for sewing seams.

Sewing Piping in a Seam

Measure the perimeter of the pillow front and add 3", then cut the piping to this measurement. Place the pillow front right side up. Position the piping at the center of one edge, then match the raw edges. Using a zipper foot,

machine-baste the piping to the front cover along the previous machine-basting lines. To turn the corners, stop sewing about $1^1/2$" from the corner. Leave the needle in the down position in the fabric. Lift the zipper foot and, using sharp scissors, clip into the piping casing almost to the stitching line several times at short intervals. Lower the foot and resume sewing, easing the piping in a gentle curve (D).

Continue sewing the piping all around the pillow edge until you are 2" from the starting point—stop with the needle in the down position. Trim the excess piping 1" beyond the starting point, then pick out the basting stitches for $2^1/2$". Trim the cable cord so it butts the cord at the starting point. Fold the short fabric end $1/2$" to the inside. Pick out the basting stitches at the starting point and slide the folded end underneath the piping (E). Wrap the fabric around the beginning section and continue

A

B

C

Sewing a Ruffle in a Seam

Place the pillow front right side up on a flat surface and mark the center of each edge with a pin (B). Pin the ruffle to the pillow front, matching the pins and the raw edges. Adjust the gathers to fit each pillow section, and allow extra fullness at the corners (C). Machine-baste the ruffle to the pillow $1/2$" from the edge between the gathering stitches. Assemble the pillow as usual.

Lace

Lace is either sold flat or pregathered by the yard. Machine-baste flat lace and draw it up as you would a fabric ruffle. Flat lace can be placed on top of a fabric ruffle, and the two can be gathered up together.

Fringe

Wool, cotton, rayon, and silk fringes complement a variety of pillow styles. Most fringes are sewn in the seams of the pillow following the piping method. If the braid or tape connecting the fringe is especially pretty, hand-stitch the fringe to the edge of the finished pillow instead.

Tassels

Tassels are frequently seen dangling from the corners of plump knife-edged pillows. To secure them in the seam during assembly, pin each tassel to the right side of the pillow front so the end passes over the corner and the tassel extends diagonally toward the center of the pillow. Sew the seam as usual, but be careful to clip just the corner, not the tassel end. If the end is long enough, knot it for extra security after sewing.

machine-basting to secure all layers. Assemble the pillow as usual, stitching slightly to the left of the machine basting.

Ruffles

Ruffles add a flouncy, feminine touch to knife-edged pillows. Ruffles look complicated, but they are actually simple rectangles that can be cut lengthwise, crosswise, or on the bias of the fabric. Bias cuts can be especially attractive on striped and plaid fabrics.

Making a Ruffle Decide on a finished ruffle width (for most pillow sizes, 3"–6" is appropriate). Cut a fabric strip that is 2 times the width plus 1" and $2\frac{1}{2}$ to 3 times the pillow perimeter, depending on the fullness desired. Sew the short ends of the strip together, right sides facing, and press the seam open. You should have a continuous fabric loop. Fold the loop in half lengthwise, right side out, pressing as you go; the pressed fold is the outer edge of the ruffle. Machine-baste $3/8$" and again $5/8$" from the raw edges through both layers. Insert four straight pins perpendicular to the basting stitches to divide the ruffle into four equal segments (A). Carefully pull the ends of the bobbin basting threads, gathering the raw edge until it equals the perimeter of the pillow. Tie the thread ends in a bow to prevent the gathers from slipping. Do not use a knot, in case you need to untie the ends to make an adjustment.

The chapters that follow illustrate the boundless role pillows play in making our homes more decorative as well as more comfortable. You will see pillows in traditional and cosmopolitan settings, elegant, poetic pillows in a yesteryear mode, and pillows with artistic spunk. Regardless of the style of your present or future home, or the size of your budget, you will find inspiration for pillows that you can make to enhance and complement the decor. Appreciating that a pillow looks "right" is just a first step toward successful pillow design. In the pages that follow, you will discover an exciting variety of ways in which the many elements of pillowmaking—shape, size, fabrics, trims, stuffing, sewing techniques—work together. The creative possibilities are virtually endless. Hopefully, as you draw inspiration from the photographs and captions, you will develop an eye for those special details that go beyond the ordinary and learn how to incorporate them into magnificent pillow designs that are truly your own.

Living Classics

MAKING AND BREAKING TRADITION

*I*nspired by a century's worth of living rooms, home libraries, garden rooms, and bedrooms, the legacy of classic pillows is always close at hand in traditional home decor. Sewn from beautiful, high-quality fabrics, classic pillows never lose sight of their function—to make an interior and its occupants feel more comfortable and relaxed. Today's favorite decorator classics include floral chintz pillows with English country house roots, retro prints from the 1930s and 1940s, and deep lounging cushions covered with silk shantung or natural unbleached linen in the International style. These time-honored styles

have given way to quirky, colorful, innovative offspring that display the same traditional tailoring but use more casual fabrics and trims. Both generations carry themselves with dignity and aplomb.

More substantial than skimpy throw pillows or floppy cushions, the typical classic pillow is firmly stuffed, large enough to lean back against, and remarkably resilient. Classic pillows specialize in clean lines and uncluttered silhouettes, making them excellent first projects for beginning sewers. Details such as braids and tassels should be kept simple so that they don't become persnickety or overdone. Finely tailored flanges, boxed corners, and welting can be easily incorporated using straight-line sewing.

The photographs in this section show the range of today's classic pillow styles, from the most formal to the most casual. Whether you make or buy one pillow or a set of half a dozen, you will find helpful hints and design ideas that demonstrate the versatility of classic style.

Left: When furniture is arranged into several separate seating areas, pillows that can circulate freely among them make a room more comfortable and inviting. The secret is a background of coordinating upholstery prints, applied in various combinations that avoid the "matched set" syndrome.

Opposite: The combination of a kaleidoscopic print and jewel-toned, solid-color fabrics is just the costume an old cast-off sofa needs to masquerade in style. When a group of orphaned, mismatched pillows were covered with the same print and layered across the sofa back, no one was any the wiser. To make sure the ensemble would come across as one piece, an eye-popping welting made from black and white striped fabric was enclosed in all of the seams. Cutting the welting strips across the fabric grain created an instant checked effect.

~

Right: Placing two matching pillows on a living room love seat proved to be the easiest, most effective way to highlight the symmetry of twin bookcases in the dining room beyond. Even though the furnishings are casual, the mirror-image placement promotes a strong underlying formality. The pillows were sewn from printed upholstery fabric that is lighter in color and slightly smaller in scale than the black print chosen for the love seat. These characteristics, together with the pillows' low rectangular profile, make the love seat appear larger than it actually is and add visual interest to the room as a whole. The short edges of the pillows are trimmed with fluffy chenille fringe.

24

~

~

Left: The three square print pillows lined up across the back of this red upholstered settee made it look too prim and proper, so they were pushed aside to make room for two exotic rectangular interlopers. The pillows are arranged in a crescent to immediately envelop and pamper anyone who sits down. Dark, rich background colors help anchor the exciting jumble of patterns on the settee and oriental rug.

$\mathcal{L}e\!\mathit{ft}\!:$ In a room without curtains, silk drapery cords make their appearance wrapped around two striped pillows instead. This unexpected touch was achieved by tying each cord in a loose bow at the top of the pillow and allowing the tassels to cascade down onto the chair cushion. The small needlepoint pillows are thoughtful accents that seated persons can prop behind them should the cords become uncomfortable to lean against. The delicate script alphabets and floral borders were hand-stitched with Persian yarns on canvas following a chart and color key.

25

~

Opposite: Who says classic has to be staid? This antique-filled bedroom is anything but rigid, thanks to an array of beautiful pillows with eclectic trimmings that wrap around each chosen fabric like an elegant picture frame. The key to harmony in this colorful setup is that the fabrics are all muted in tone and display flowers or other vegetation.

~

Right: Sofas, like people, can get the blahs. There was nothing structurally wrong with this simple white upholstered sofa and matching pillows—it's just that everybody on the block had practically the same thing! Inspired by the colors of the woven Native American rug, the owner zipped things up by stitching yards of thick moss fringe around the pillow edges, with enough left over to embellish the smaller cranberry duo that hopped on board.

~

Opposite: Turning a lineup of crushed linen pillows on point lightens up an oversized sofa when the days turn hot and muggy. To prevent the all-white summer slipcover look from becoming predictable and stilted, two gray accent pillows sewn from vintage damask fabric were introduced into the grouping. All of the pillows are easy-to-sew knife-edged styles that zip on and off for cleaning. The small cushion resting against the sofa arm has a very delicate ribbon edging sewn into the seam all around.

~

Above: A flared-arm sofa and matching tasseled pillows were elegant, but lacked zest. Two new silk pillows, one pale peach and the other taupe, proved to be perfect companions. Their smooth, shimmering surfaces show up all the more when placed against the nubby, textured wool upholstery, and their spiraled cord edgings echo the deep bullion fringe dangling below. The cord is a special type, manufactured with a fabric tape along one edge that can be enclosed in the pillow seams.

~

Right: When stacked double-height, these chunky oversized lounging cushions make an instant informal table base. Each cushion was custom-made from a block of high-density foam padded with yards of cotton batting. To keep things simple yet elegant, the covers were sewn from prequilted fabric that matches the room's bedding. Soft Turkish corners were tied securely on the wrong side of the fabric before the pillow forms were inserted.

~

Opposite: Squiggly stripes mimic the curves of a kidney-shaped sofa and glass palette coffee table in a 1950s-inspired living room. For decorating interest and to keep the design from appearing staid, the pillows are slightly different in size. The printed cotton duck fabric is long-wearing and washable.

~

Below: Deep, soft pillows in straightforward fabrics make the angular furnishings in a city living room more inviting without diminishing the cosmopolitan style. The beige pillows were tailored with a color-matched cording, and the brown and white striped pillow was sewn from ticking, a durable household fabric traditionally used to cover bed pillows and mattresses. Punching the pillows down in the center demonstrates the heft of the feather and down stuffing inside.

31
~

~

Above: Authentic—rather than eclectic—pieces sometimes make the more appropriate accessories. For these sophisticated Art Deco chairs and hassocks in mint condition, pillows styled from recycled 1930s drapery fabric were the perfect choice. The foliage print lends a homey touch to the streamlined velvet upholstery. Each pillow was lightly stuffed, allowing a covered button to be sewn clear through the center in the style of hand-tufted upholstery.

~

$\mathcal{B}$ *elow*: *An understated collection of cream and taupe striped pillows carries the eye around a peaceful, elegantly furnished living room. To avoid any jarring lines that would disrupt the tranquility, the pillow fronts and backs were carefully measured and cut so that the stripes lined up at the seams. If striped fabric is not slippery, it is possible to cut the pillow front first and use it as a pattern to cut a perfectly matched back.*

~

Left: In an entry hall that receives heavy family traffic, the pillows and seat cushion for a pickled pine bench needed to be extra tough. A striped linen and cotton blend in neutral tones was a good choice, as it is both long-wearing and washable. The corners of the bench cushion were boxed—sewn diagonally across on the inside—to fit snugly around the foam filler pad without a separate boxing strip. Fabric straps sewn into the back corners of the seat cushion tie on to the bench posts to prevent slippage.

~

Left: Swedish-inspired blue and white stripes make a room feel open, airy, and summery year-round and eliminate all those hard-to-face color decisions when all you really need is a little serenity. In a move toward simplicity, the pillows in this quiet conversation corner were sewn from the same fabric used to cover the walls. The boxing strips were cut on the crosswise grain of the fabric so that the stripes lined up at the top and bottom of the pillow but ran perpendicular at the sides. A large monogram was machine-embroidered on the face of each pillow in silky white thread.

~

$\mathcal{O}_{pposite:}$ *Sometimes elegance does not spell comfort, as was the case with these deep settee and chair frames that made real repose against the back cushions impossible. The solution: a flank of knife-edged pillows that march across the seat cushions in parade-ground order. The solid pink, violet, and mauve fabrics make the furniture stand out, unlike before when the upholstery print, though pretty, was dwarfed by the mammoth portico.*

~

$\mathcal{B}_{elow:}$ *Just an armful of sunny yellow pillows prevents this green-house-turned-gathering-room from becoming too shady and junglelike. The roof was painted white to block scorching rays that could overheat the glass enclosure. To compensate for the loss of direct overhead sunlight and to balance the intensity of the surrounding greenery, the yellow pillows were brought in to work their cheery magic.*

~

$\mathcal{A}_{bove:}$ *At a seaside vacation retreat, home furnishings fabrics should be fuss-free, good-looking, and inexpensive. Here, an unpretentious mix of solid-color and pastel-striped cotton pillows add comfort and charm and promise easy living. Durable, washable, and okay-not-to-iron, the pillows are ready to prop behind a tired head when a daytime snooze is in order.*

~

Below: An L-shaped sofa banked with pillows of many fabrics and colors forms an exciting candy-colored collection. To prevent the colors in the room from becoming overwhelming, two design motifs—diamonds and stripes—help to keep everything related. Diamonds show up on the quilted cushion and pillow fabrics, echoing the painted wall treatment and the pink upholstered chair in partial view at the right. Striped pillows play off the lines of the unusual beech bentwood chair in the foreground. At the rear of the sofa is the room's single multicolor pillow, sewn from a dazzling abstract print.

~

Left: Architectural built-ins that are seldom used may be candidates for a little pillow therapy. This pantry window seat had a lovely view of the garden, but everybody complained that the spot lacked warmth and that the seat was too hard. A trio of thick seat cushions and matching pillows solved the problem beautifully. The bright tropical foliage print livens up the area, and the pillows camouflage the dead space in the corners to make the seat cozier. The cushions overhang the bench slightly, so that the hard edge doesn't dig into the backs of knees.

37
~

~

Right: You know that old wicker rocker sitting on the porch—the one with the seat that's too low? It may just be missing its seat cushion. These twin rockers are just the right height now that they have replacement seat cushions just as thick as the early twentieth-century originals. Tie-on backrests and large knife-edged pillows complete the chairs' summery attire.

$\sim$

$\mathcal{A}bove:$ The rolled bolster that came with this formal white upholstered daybed was fine as an armrest but needed some help for laid-back lounging. A set of striped canvas pillows came to the rescue, instilling comfort and a touch of whimsy. The pillows can be propped against the bolster for an impromptu backrest, and each person who uses the spot can plump them up in a personally comfortable arrangement. The reversible two-tone aqua pillow was assembled by sewing two different fabrics together; to make strong, neat joins, center seams should be first pressed open and then to one side.

$\sim$

$\mathcal{A}bove:$ Enriching one pattern by introducing others is an old decorating idea that can be a challenge to put into practice. Those just testing the waters may want to take their cues from the brown and red pillows featured here. Each was sewn from a subtle tone-on-tone print that picks up a single color from the daybed linens below. All the patterns feature swirly designs and are similar in scale, another secret to their compatibility.

~

Below: Three pastel pillows that seem to spill so artlessly across a feminine chaise were actually carefully selected and positioned to complement the upholstery's soft Grecian folds. To create the illusion of motion, the pillows are graduated in size, with the largest pillow at the back. Alternating the colors ensures that each pillow's shape will stand out—an easy way to highlight the tumble-down effect. The custom-made chair cushion at the left is curved in front and straight in back, and even has small notches to accommodate the chair arms. The form was made using a paper template cut to fit the chair seat.

~

Right: To better show off the sleek lines of a contemporary sleigh
bed, the bedding was deliberately kept low-key, with the
accent on fine tailoring rather than flashy colors. The square pillow
forms are a European size that is available through most
bedding retailers. Pure cotton fabric ensures that the flanges retain
their stiff, just-starched look even through repeated washings.

~

Left: Black and white
are a legendary pair,
unsurpassed for their clarity
and drama. Here, a
bedroom's entire color
scheme is paraphrased
by two white pillows edged
with black fringe.

41

~

Above: When the garden view is this lovely, there is no need to overdress the
porch furniture. The khaki cushions and bolsters sewn for an ample bamboo
sofa frame are long-wearing, serviceable, and sumptuously squashy. To achieve a
softer appearance, the bolster edges were lightly gathered before the piping
and pancake ends were sewn into place.

~

Opposite: Diverse patterns that share colors in common enjoy a
lively conversation on a hand-caned settee. The party includes
an allover rust-on-white print, an oriental peach silk, a deep gold batik
fabric, and a cream and gold floral print. Behind the group and
partially concealed is a bold orange and violet striped pillow. None of
the colors used here match exactly, but their camaraderie shows
that they all speak the same language; they are totally compatible.

~

Above: A dainty bolster befits a settee with feminine curves.
The excess fabric at the end of the bolster was carefully drawn
in toward the center to created the soft petal-like folds. The holding
stitches are concealed with a matching fabric-covered button.

~

PART TWO

Heirloom Pillows

THE VOICE OF NOSTALGIA

*J*ust three or four generations ago, the homemaker who put her needlework on display was not simply decorating her parlor—she was basking in her household's prosperity. Fine white-on-white embroidery, pictorial Berlin woolwork, and crocheted lace trims represented hours of leisure stitching time. A middle-class home adorned with such handwork was considered the pinnacle of nineteenth-century domestic achievement, celebrating the teamwork of a successful breadwinner husband and a wife who presided over the family's budget, meals, linens, and housekeeping—with time to spare.

Today, elegant old stitchery is being rediscovered for its beauty, subtlety, and the human touch it brings to both period and contemporary decor.

To capture this heirloom look, designers are incorporating the undamaged sections of old hand-stitched linens, tapestries, and garments into nostalgic pillow covers. Textiles with printed or woven designs augment the look. Many high-quality, natural-fiber fabrics were manufactured in the early twentieth century for use as slipcovers, draperies, table linens, and bedspreads. Faded by a half century or more of sunshine and repeated washings, they impart instant lineage to the pillows sewn from them. Hunting down samples of old needlework and fabric yardage for pillowmaking requires a bit of legwork at untraditional fabric shopping sources, such as rummage sales, estate auctions, and flea markets. The search is always well worth the extra effort when a special piece is found.

The photographs collected in this section show the many possibilities when old—and old-looking—textiles are sewn into pillow covers. In a rapidly changing world, the decor that respects and showcases these pillows gains an aura of history and serenity that, for brief moments, makes time stand still.

~

Left: In this cozy bedroom, two all-cotton pillowcases are trimmed with exquisite hand-crocheted edgings—true heirloom possessions. The envelope-style pillow cover next to the bed pillows is embroidered with blue satin stitch. In the background, scalloped percale borders and gold braid dress up a group of shams sewn from utilitarian striped ticking. The nostalgic bed coverlet is assembled from printed cotton hankies from the 1930s and 1940s.

~

Opposite: Exquisitely detailed laces used in fine French hand sewing add a demure touch to three cotton percale pillow covers. New methods for applying the laces by sewing machine have brought this exciting hand-worked look within reach of anyone who sews. The flat pillow fronts are small and easy to maneuver, making them the perfect beginner's project.

45

~

~

Right: Once the seat
cushion is made for an alcove
window bench, decorative
accent pillows can be added
at a leisurely pace. In this
case, the pillows pick up on
the room's red and white floral
theme, on both the stenciled
built-in closet and the drapery.
The white pillow ringed
with realistic fabric roses and
leaves is a special project.
Alongside are rectangular
pillows embroidered with red
candlewicking, an easy technique that works up fast. The
posy print pillows are tempo-
rary fillers until the occupant
of this bedroom completes
another pillow creation.

46

~

Right: Putting yesteryear's linens in contemporary settings
is one way to enjoy elements of the past without sacrificing the clean
lines and easy-care routines of the present. The pillow shams
in this twenty-first-century bedroom feature old-fashioned scalloped
flanges that can be duplicated using a computerized sewing
machine. When the machine embroidery was completed, the excess
fabric was trimmed away with small, sharp embroidery scissors
to reveal the delicate curves.

~

Left: Two bolsters made for a slipcovered couch have the
same size form inside, but the similarities end there. The bolster at
the edge of the couch was sewn with an extra-long fabric allowance
at the end, which was gathered together and tied with a tasseled
cord. The other, a variation on the pancake-end bolster, has a
flirtatious flounce around the edges that mimics the slipcover skirt.
The envelope-style pillow cover was sewn from a demure cotton
print and trimmed with pink piping and cream tassels; its knife-edged
pillow form slips right out when the cover needs laundering.

$\mathcal{O}_{pposite:}$ A small piece of woven tapestry fabric, left over after the drapes were sewn, makes a lovely accent pillow for a master bedroom. The drapes were hung print side facing the street, giving the pillow center stage indoors. Its graceful flower and leaf pattern is accented by a rustling taffeta bed skirt that spills generously onto the floor. Behind the pillow, a white linen bolster with poufed ends spans the width of the bed, adding warmth and comfort.

$\mathcal{B}_{elow:}$ A special manufacturing technique gave these vintage round pillow fabrics their slightly raised and puckered appearance, for the look of finely detailed embroidery. The silk boxing strips were cut three times the customary length, then pleated all around before being joined to the pillow fronts and backs.

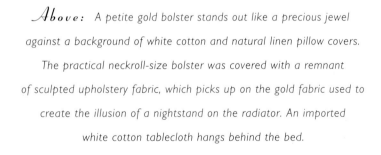

$\mathcal{A}_{bove:}$ A petite gold bolster stands out like a precious jewel against a background of white cotton and natural linen pillow covers. The practical neckroll-size bolster was covered with a remnant of sculpted upholstery fabric, which picks up on the gold fabric used to create the illusion of a nightstand on the radiator. An imported white cotton tablecloth hangs behind the bed.

~

Above: A change of heart doesn't have to lead to full-scale redecorating — it can often be satisfied by pillows in a new style. When the occupant of a traditional, tailored bedroom began yearning for more elegant surroundings, two brocade pillows gracefully made their appearance. Their quiet blush and gently sculpted pattern helped ease the transition and even inspired the purchase of a new duvet cover with subtle white-on-white foliage. Romantic details include silk tassels and long fringe.

~

Below: Mellowing a contemporary black and white interior with old printed fabrics is an approach many have used successfully, but these pillows go a step further. Each one was trimmed with a scant pleated ruffle that adds a feminine counterpoint to the room's overall masculine ambience. Other details to note are the sculpted white pillow cover, sewn from an old bedspread, and the small rectangular pillow's single-button closure.

~

Left: Once a fancy slipcover or long dining room drapes, this muted blue and beige ruffled pillow sham adds a feeling of warmth to a sparsely adorned reading corner, perhaps reminding its beach house occupants of an earlier family home. The floral pattern echoes that of the upholstery and is a nice counterpoint to all of the white surfaces and bright light in the room. The sham closes in front with a single dark blue button.

51

~

Right: Pillows offered for sale in a nostalgia shop are easily duplicated by the home sewer who has imagination and vision. Old printed chintzes naturally lend themselves to pillows with ruffled trims and decorative cording. The petite maroon velvet cushion is an elegant idea for a remnant of expensive fabric. The large rectangular tapestry cushion is a rare find—it was assembled from an old piano seat cover.

~

Below: When the furniture in a room is old and eclectic in origin, the pillows should be, too. Sewn over a period of time from assorted fabrics, the pillows on a massive daybed are textile treasures, each one adding its own tantalizing story to the decor. Together, they create a cozy, comfortable corner for reading or lounging.

~

Above: A deep olive chair forms the perfect backdrop for a pair of crimson velvet pillows, an example of placing opposing colors together for heightened contrast. Each pillow's patterned center panel, taken from worn-out draperies or perhaps an old fabric bellpull, imparts a touch of the past to a resoundingly contemporary apartment.

~

Right: A creative, thrifty soul used just a few remnants of natural and floral-print linen—none of them large enough to sew even a single pillow—to make a family of pillows for a wicker daybed. The face of each pillow was assembled patchwork style by cutting and fitting different-size pieces of fabric together. Some of the linen strips cut for the project were shirred before the seams were joined. The large white pillows in the background were edged with a gathered ruffle casing that was threaded with a heavy cord for added shape and volume.

~

Left: The large printed patterns found on vintage drapery and tablecloth fabrics lend themselves beautifully to pillow covers. Here, a simple flange-edged pillow sham shows off a faded floral bouquet salvaged from cotton drapes, while the pillow next to it displays the bouquet more broadly and was bordered with jumbo piping. The blue pillow was hand-stitched in needlepoint.

~

Signature Accents

PILLOWS WITH PERSONALITY

Sooner or later, an unusual, out-of-the-ordinary pillow will suggest itself to you. You may be inspired by a particular color, some beads you see in a shop, or a textile find at a flea market. Some designs emerge instantly in swift geyserlike explosions, while others develop slowly through experimentation and quiet searching for just the right material or embellishment. When you treat the pillow form as a blank canvas, anything you can envision in your mind's eye is certainly fair game for your creative efforts.

Many intriguing pillows make inventive use of the sewing machine. Textural effects include pleats, machine-sewn passementerie, and patchwork. Other embellishments such as buttons, pearls, and beads require patient hand sewing. Surface decoration methods include appliqué, batik, stenciling, fabric painting, silk screen, and photo-transfer printing. When you find a technique that you would like to try for the first time, thinking about it in terms of a pillow cover will help you keep the project small and manageable.

Like people, pillows that demonstrate wit, inventiveness, and a sense of exploration are most welcome guests in our homes. Their sparkle and zest is contagious and worth emulating.

~

Left: The owner of this bedroom-turned-art-gallery covered the luminous silk pillows here in primary colors—red, yellow, and blue—that showed off the squiggles, dashes, and crisscrossed lines hand-painted on top. For washability later on, fabrics should be decorated with textile paints (the ones used here glow in the dark) and allowed to dry thoroughly before the pillow covers are cut and sewn.

~

Opposite: The lively pillows shown here were assembled from purchased embroidered panels that repeat indigenous designs, yet remain delightfully unique. The arrangement of colors on this iron daybed demonstrates again how seemingly disparate fabrics can work together if they are of the same color intensity.

~

Right: In the quest for
exotic fabrics, it's important
not to overlook the common-
place. An Indian cotton
print bedspread, purchased
inexpensively at an import
store, was the fabric source for
the black and gold pillows
sequestered in this tropical
hideaway. Cutting the pillow
pieces from different sections
of the bedspread yielded
the asymmetrical pattern
placement. The deep brown
and white pillow cover shows
thread-dyed motifs.

Above: A printed slipcover or drapery fabric can often inspire an artistic interpretation to go with it. This bright floral slipcover is complemented by a hand-painted aqua pillow that will never lose its distinctive edge over commercially produced pretenders. The pink pillows to each side have gently shirred boxing strips that echo the fabric's soft striations. The gold floral pillows are part of the slipcover set.

Right: Any type of brushstroke art, from tole painting to Norway's rosemaling, can be adapted to painting on fabric. This oriental medallion on red fabric shows the swirls and blended shading characteristic of the brushstroke motion. The pillow backing is dark blue fabric, and a blue and white twisted cord decorates the seam. The brilliant red color is all the more striking displayed against a white cotton pillow edged with crocheted pineapple lace.

Left: Combing the thrift shops for textiles that have pillowmaking potential can yield some exciting bargain finds—like the panel of colorful triangles shown here. Each triangle is set off from its neighbors by creamy chenille embroidery. The pillow front was enlarged by stitching strips of a flowery print fabric to each side. All in all, the owner ended up with an artsy accent for about the same price as a more ordinary cover.

Right: Patchwork is made by cutting fabric into different shapes and sizes and sewing the pieces together. These "pineapple" patchwork pillows were made from strips, stitched in sequence so that the pattern builds from the center out. The crisp overlaps and points that resulted resemble the outer skin of a fresh pineapple, giving the pattern its name. The finished patchwork block was framed with wide fabric strips cut from the same fabric as the pillowback.

Left: Pillow art that indulges a pet passion gives a bedroom unbounded personality. This animal lover's private retreat revels in pictures of pampered pets, including a winsome spaniel portrait surrounded by delicate tucks and a vine wreath. Cheerful borders decorate the edges of the pet pillows, and more intriguing pillows peek out from behind to complete the scene.

59

~

Below: A teal mattress and coordinating pillows turn an under-the-stairs reading nook into an artistic hot spot. Sewn from easy-care cotton fabrics, the pillows introduce instant color in a small space and can be re-covered in new colors whenever the owners want to change the look.

~

Above: On a creamy neutral couch, two artistic pillows stand out as clearly as colorful paintings on a white wall. A band of printed decorator fabric wraps around the simple duffle-style bolster casing— different sections of the print show depending on which way the bolster is turned. The round tuffet was assembled from a long rectangle of striped fabric. Like the bolster, the excess fabric was gathered into a tight circle on each side. The gathering cords and casings on both front and back are concealed by jumbo covered buttons.

~

Right: A colorful geometric design looks like patchwork but is actually a printed textile. Since the repeats on this bold designer print fabric are spaced far apart, the fabric cuts had to be carefully planned so that all the pillow fronts would be identical.

~

Left: Patchwork sewing is the mastermind behind many fun optical effects, like the red and white striped pinwheel that's spinning along here. The back of this novelty pillow cover was sewn to match, and small yellow ties tacked near the corners were used to secure both pieces around a muslin-covered pillow form. The companion pillow features fabric squares appliquéd to plain muslin.

61
~

Below: A striking pillow lineup illustrates the possibilities when patchwork techniques are applied to sophisticated, neutral-toned fabrics. The patchwork pieces are large, so each pillow front involved only a few seams. The patterns were drafted with seam allowances from actual-size drawings. The pillow edges were trimmed with either textured moss fringe or piping.

~

Above: When a touch of glamour, à la Hollywood, is called for, it doesn't hurt to go for the glitz. Here, an accent pillow's light-catching gold and bronze metallic threads are exceptionally beautiful. The thread-dyed design, depicting scenes and flowers from an oriental garden, was woven rather than printed on the fabric. The small pillow size keeps this expensive fabric affordable.

~

Above: Grouping pillows by theme makes for confident decorating, even when only a few furnishings are involved. A small bombé chest, faux marble walls, and trumpeting angel inspired the Renaissance-Baroque flavor of a spare bedroom. The pillows carried through on the historical theme, using white heraldic crests on a blue field, gold braid appliqués on velvet, and a miniature leopard print that suggests trade caravans from exotic lands.

~

Left: Marking pens specially designed for use on textiles can be used to create "signature" fabrics that mimic printed designer originals. Sources for historic signatures include biographies, facsimile editions and reprints, copies of historic documents, and books on handwriting analysis. After the signatures are enlarged, they can be transferred to fabric by tracing over a light box. The collected signatures of your own friends and family can be equally as effective—and more personal.

64

~

Right: There's no rule that says pictures must be surrounded by frames and hung on the wall. These lifelike monkeys, copied from zoological engravings, were silk-screened by a professional artist on cotton fabric. A similar effect can be produced by a high-quality photocopy or tee-shirt printing shop using any clear photograph or illustration. Once the designs are printed, they can be assembled with other fabrics to create an attractive pillow collage.

~

Above: This pillow's coarse hessianlike background fabric suggests
it may have started off as a utilitarian overseas shipping bag.
Merchants, manufacturers, and shippers imprinted their packaging
with identifying logos and insignias, such as the memorable leopard
and majestic palm image shown here.

~

Right: Geometric designs normally glimpsed underfoot take on new life when thread-bare kilim rugs are recycled into pillows. The pillow shown here features border rows from the rug's edges, which typically show better condition than the faster-wearing center. Velvet and sueded cotton are appropriate fabric choices for a pillow back when the front is a heavy material, such as a rug or needlepoint canvas. A sharp, heavy-duty sewing machine needle helps pierce through the dense rug fibers, though the pieces can also be sewn by hand using a crewel needle and strong thread. Other pillows in the group include a dog print edged in multicolor fringe, a pink and white pastoral print with self-ruffle, and a fresh ivy print. The 1920s yo-yo coverlet was assembled from hundreds of colorful fabric circles.

66

~

~

Below: Woven wool camp blankets offer eye-catching colors and designs for novelty western-style pillows. The same fabrics were used for the pillow fronts and backs, making the pillows totally reversible. To prevent soft, loose blanket weaves from puckering or pulling during sewing, the sewing machine is fitted with a ball-point needle, which separates rather than pierces the fibers.

~

Above: When two similarly patterned pillows serendipitously turned up, displaying them next to each other didn't quite work. One pillow was sewn from a high-quality woven textile (right), which made the coarser-textured hand-knit intarsia adaptation (left) appear inadequate in comparison. Placing the pillows across from each other on a daybed resolved the problem. The pillow designs play off each other, and each one is appreciated for what it is.

67

68

Left: Smaller pillows were always falling off this armless banquette, so its owner devised a long, slender cushion that spanned the entire seat and was guaranteed to stay put. The cushion fabric's brown and white woven stripes prove a handsome and contemporary match for the striped banquette. A backing of plush chenille (another ploy to reduce slipping) peeks around the edges.

Opposite: Even the most simple striped fabric can turn interesting corners. Dark green stripes stretch out to the max on a metal frame chaise, then rearrange themselves in a square to make the bull's-eye cushion. The cushion's secret is four identical triangles, sewn together on the diagonal.

Sources

Materials and Supplies

Fabric, thread, and trims for pillowmaking are available at sewing supply stores, in fabric departments in large retail stores, at warehouse and mill end outlets, and by mail. You can identify sources in your area by consulting your local telephone directory. Mail-order sources can be found through advertisements in fashion, home decorating, and sewing magazines. Depending on the type of store, you may find bolts of fabric neatly arranged at eye level, rolls of fabric stacked three or four deep on wide shelves, or loose cuts of fabric in bins. Bargains abound, if you know what you are looking for. End cuts of expensive fabrics are often a perfect size for pillowmaking and are sold at a discount of the same fabric bought off the bolt.

Old, used textiles, including lace edgings, needlepoint, and embroidered panels, turn up at flea markets, tag and estate sales, rummage sales, and thrift shops. Affordable substitutes for vintage handwork are new crocheted doilies, hand-appliquéd tea towels, Battenberg lace table linens, and similar pieces imported from Asia, all of which are usually sold in bedding and home furnishings stores.

Stuffing materials are sold in several places, depending on the type. Spun-polyester pillow forms, fiberfill, and batting are available at full-service fabric and craft retailers, variety stores, and wherever sewing notions are sold. High-density foam is sold at foam suppliers, which can be located through the telephone directory; when you call, ask the shop if it will cut foam to size for you. Down and feathers can be purchased through bedding suppliers, who can also clean and fluff up natural fillings from old pillows that you wish to recycle.

General sewing supplies, such as scissors, needles, and pins, are sold at mass merchandise stores, variety stores, and many fabric stores (though generally not at discount warehouse outlets, which specialize only in fabric). Fabric shops catering to quilters are a good source for rotary cutters and accessories, and local shops often sponsor small-group instruction to help beginners get started.

Design Ideas

Fresh, new design ideas for pillowmaking abound in the pages of decorating magazines, home furnishings catalogs, and department store flyers. Pillows are used so universally that even feature articles about other furnishings, or about a home's decoration in general, will contain interesting photographs of them. Other sources include store displays, consumer-oriented decorating shows, the homes or public places you visit in the course of your day, and even the stage sets seen in films and television programs. When you see a good idea "on the run," draw a small sketch and jot down a few of the pertinent features—for example, "Round, red velvet, seven gold braid fleur-de-lis appliqués"—so that you can recall the design later on.

If you find you are having trouble figuring out what style is right for your home, try setting up a file folder and dropping in pictures of pillows that you like as you come across them in your magazines and catalogs. Do this for several months, then take a look at the pictures you've assembled. You are sure to see a pattern in your choices that will help you define your design direction.

Reading

For current articles on pillowmaking techniques and fabrics, consult your local public library or newsstand for home decor and needlework magazines that emphasize a hands-on approach. Two excellent, though out-of-print, sources for pillowmaking techniques beyond the scope of this book are listed below. Your local public librarian or used book dealer may be able to obtain them for you or locate others on the subject.

Burgess, Maureen. *The Pillow Book*. New York: Grosset & Dunlap, 1975.

How to Make Pillows. Menlo Park, Calif.: Lane Publishing Co., 1981 [a *Sunset* book].

Index

~

Conversion
Chart for
Common
Measurements
~

The following chart lists the approximate metric equivalents of inch measurements up to 20", rounded for practical use. To calculate equivalents not listed, multiply the number of inches by 2.54cm. To convert 36", for example, multiply 36 times 2.54, for an equivalent of 91.44cm, or 91.5cm when rounded.

¹/₂" = 1.3cm	
1" = 2.5cm	11" = 28cm
2" = 5cm	12" = 30.5cm
3" = 7.5cm	13" = 33cm
4" = 10cm	14" = 35.5cm
5" = 12.5cm	15" = 38cm
6" = 15cm	16" = 40.5cm
7" = 18cm	17" = 43cm
8" = 20.5cm	18" = 45.5cm
9" = 23cm	19" = 48cm
10" = 25.5cm	20" = 51cm

*P*hotography *C*redits

Courtesy of Ballard Designs/
    Atlanta, Georgia: 64 (both)
©Grey Crawford: 6, 27, 30, 31
    (bottom), 54, 63 (right), 69
©Phillip Ennis: 9, 24 (both),
    26, 35, 40 (left), 47 (left), 52
    (bottom), 63 (left)
©Feliciano: 21, 23, 28 (bottom),
    57 (top)

©Michael Garland: 37 (top),
    45, 61 (top), 65, 67 (left), 68
    (bottom)
©Tria Giovan: 2, 29, 34 (top), 37
    (bottom), 38 (left), 42, 48
    (top), 58 (top), 67 (right)
©Mick Hales: 28 (top), 41, 43, 52
    (top), 59, 66
©images/Dennis Krukowski: 49,
    57 (bottom)

©David Livingston: 8, 25, 38
    (right), 60 (top), 61 (bottom)
©Richard Mandelkorn: 7, 18
©Randy O'Rourke: 40 (right)
©David Phelps: 32, 33 (top),
    48 (bottom), 50 (top), 53
    (bottom)
©Eric Roth: 33 (bottom), 39
©Bill Rothschild: 12, 46, 62

©Tim Street-Porter: 22, 31 (top),
    34 (bottom), 36, 44, 47 (right),
    50 (right), 51 (both), 53 (top),
    55, 56, 60 (bottom), 68 (top)

Drawings: ©Barbara Hennig, 1994